More Knock Knock JOKES

A Buddy Book
by **Ima Laffin**

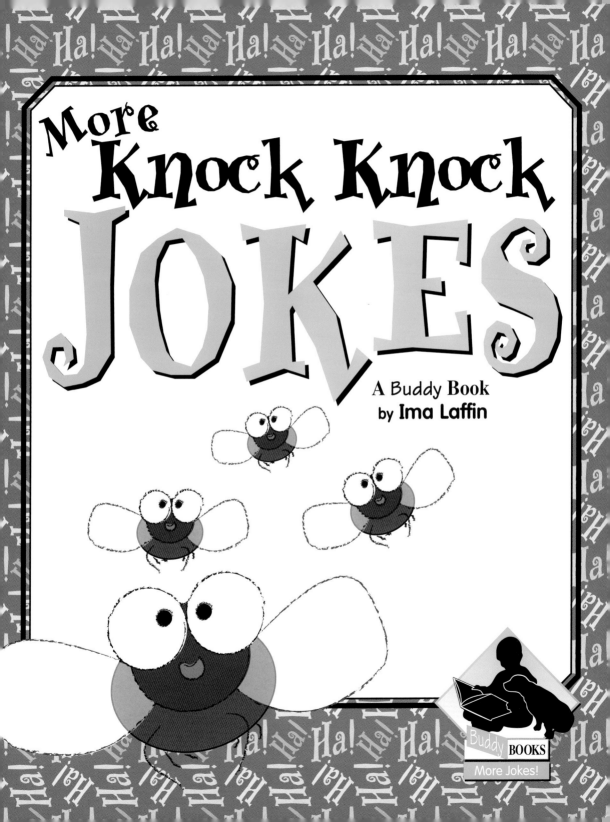

Buddy BOOKS

More Jokes!

VISIT US AT
www.abdopub.com

Published by ABDO Publishing Company, 4940 Viking Drive, Suite 622, Edina, Minnesota 55435.
Copyright © 2005 by Abdo Consulting Group, Inc. International copyrights reserved in all countries. No
part of this book may be reproduced in any form without written permission from the publisher.

Printed in the United States.

Edited by: Sarah Tieck
Contributing Editors: Jeff Lorge, Michael P. Goecke
Graphic Design: Deborah Coldiron
Illustrations by: Deborah Coldiron and Maria Hosley

Library of Congress Cataloging-in-Publication Data

Laffin, Ima, 1970-
  More knock knock jokes / Ima Laffin.
      p. cm. — (More jokes!)
  Includes index.
  ISBN 1-59197-873-4
    1. Knock-knock jokes. 2. Wit and humor, Juvenile. I. Title. II. Series.

PN6231.K55L37 2005
818'.602—dc22

                                                2004055448

Knock knock! Who's there?
Tennis. Tennis who?
Tennis-see!

Knock knock! Who's there?
Ilene. Ilene who?
Ilene-d over the fence too far
and it broke!

Knock knock! Who's there?
Wilma. Wilma who?
Wilma lunch be ready soon?

Knock knock! Who's there?
Anita. Anita who?
Anita tissue! Ah choo!

Knock knock! Who's there?
Hoo. Hoo who?
You sound like an owl!

Knock knock! Who's there?
Toby. Toby Who?
Toby or not to be!

Knock knock! Who's there?
Alaska. Alaska who?
Alaska one more time!

Knock knock! Who's there?
Me. Me who?
MEOWWWWW!

Knock knock! Who's there?
Sarah. Sarah who?
Sarah 'nother way into
this building?

Knock knock! Who's there?
Donut. Donut who?
Donut let the flies in
the house!

Knock knock! Who's there?
Would. Would who?
Would you get me out of here?

Knock knock! Who's there?
Apple! Apple who?
Apple your hair if you don't
let me in!

Knock knock! Who's there?
Phyllis. Phyllis who?
Phyllis up a cup of water!

Knock knock! Who's there?
Nanny. Nanny who?
Knock knock! Who's there?
Nanny. Nanny who?
Knock knock! Who's there?
Nanny. Nanny who?
Knock knock! Who's there?
Auntie. Auntie who?
Auntie you sick of Nanny?

Knock knock! Who's there?
Water. Water who?
Water way to answer the door!

Knock knock! Who's there?
Goat. Goat who?
Goat away!

Knock knock! Who's there?
Archie. Archie-who?
God bless you!

Knock knock! Who's there?
Ben. Ben who?
Ben over and kiss me!

Knock knock! Who's there?
Boo. Boo who?
Don't cry. It's only a joke.

Knock knock! Who's there?
Isabelle. Isabelle who?
Isabelle necessary on the door?

Knock knock! Who's there?
Tank! Tank who?
You're welcome!

Knock knock! Who's there?
Tick. Tick who?
Tick 'em up. I'm a tig tad towboy!

Knock knock! Who's there?
Seville. Seville who?
Seville you play with me?

Knock knock! Who's there?
Dwayne. Dwayne who?
Dwayne the bathtub,
I'm dwowning!

Knock knock! Who's there?
Stan. Stan who?
Stan over there!

Knock knock! Who's there?
Water. Water who?
Water you answering the
door for?

Knock knock! Who's there?
Amelia! Amelia who?
Amelia a package last week—
did you get it?

Knock knock! Who's there?
Daisy! Daisy who?
Daisy plays, nights he sleeps!

Knock knock! Who's there?
Yolanda. Yolanda who?
Yolanda me some money.

Knock knock! Who's there?
Will. Will who?
Will you leave me alone?

Knock knock! Who's there?
Sonny. Sonny who?
Sonny outside isn't it!

Knock knock! Who's there?
Stan. Stan who?
Stan back, I'm knocking
the door down!

Knock knock! Who's there?
Nobel. Nobel who?
Nobel, that's why I knocked!

Knock knock! Who's there?
Hawaii. Hawaii who?
I'm fine, Hawaii you?

Knock knock! Who's there?
Cows. Cows who?
Cows go moo, not who!

Knock knock! Who's there?
Argue. Argue who?
Argue going to let me in or not?

Knock knock! Who's there?
Letter. Letter who?
Letter open the door already!

Knock knock! Who's there?
Good. Good who?
Goodbye!

Knock knock! Who's there?
Sincerely. Sincerely who?
Sincerely this morning I've been
waiting for you to open this door!

Web Sites

Visit ABDO Publishing Company on the World Wide Web. Joke Web sites for children are featured on our Book Links page. These links are monitored and updated to provide the silliest information available.

www.abdopub.com